hope
of all the
earth

AN ADVENT DEVOTIONAL

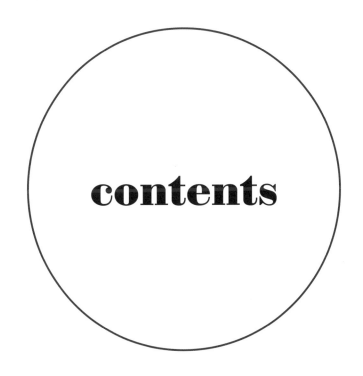

contents

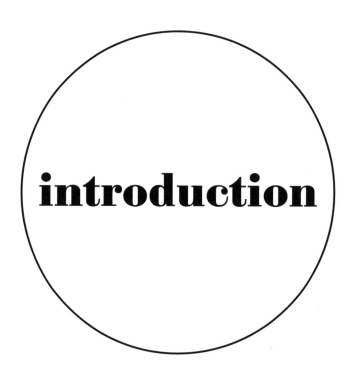

introduction

Advent is one of the great seasons of the Christian calendar. It is a season when we can look at the brokenness and fallenness of the world around us yet testify boldly and confidently, "The light shines in the darkness, and the darkness has not overcome it" (John 1:5). As we prepare to celebrate the first Advent—the first coming of Christ to this world—we also look forward to his second and final Advent, when he will come in glory to make all things once again good and very good.

Over these next weeks, we will journey together through the four great Advent themes of hope, peace, joy, and love. Advent begins on the fourth Sunday before Christmas. This year, that's November 30. As we consider and meditate on these themes of Advent, we join in celebration with the universal church for these next four Sundays. There is something deeply significant about a local faith community spending intentional time together in the same scriptures for a season. There is something even more significant about a family of local churches across a district, a region, or even the globe journeying through this season intentionally together.

Thank you for being part of this adventure. Just as he did at Bethlehem, may Christ—the very hope of all the earth—come to each of us and all of us in a way that changes everything.

—REV. DAVID GILMOUR
BRITISH ISLES

First Sunday
of Advent

hope

NOVEMBER 30, 2025

Scripture

LUKE 2:1–3

In those days Caesar Augustus issued a decree that a census should be taken of the entire Roman world. (This was the first census that took place while Quirinius was governor of Syria.) And everyone went to their own town to register.

———

During the first week of Advent, we celebrate hope—and it's easy for us to see why. Jesus Christ, the hope of all the earth, is born! Jesus is the ultimate expression of the love of God, undeniable proof that we matter, that we're precious, that we're important enough for God to become flesh and move into our neighbourhood.

The incarnation is a message of hope directly from God to humanity. God fully embraced our fallenness and fragility, our brokenness and messiness, all so we could be rescued. This is a message of incredible hope! Yet it came at a time that seemed utterly, tragically hopeless. In fact, Luke takes great care to emphasise the hopelessness of the situation. "In those days," he writes. *Those days*, when God's people were once again living in captivity and bondage. *Those days*, when worship of the one true God was openly mocked by the faith systems of imperial Rome. *Those days*, when the fate of Abraham's children was decided by emperors and governors and kings who cared nothing for Yahweh or his people.

Those days had precious little hope, and it only seemed to be getting worse. The census ordered by Caesar Augustus served a number of purposes, none of which would have inspired hope for the Jewish people. It meant more efficient taxes, which would pay for more efficient oppression. The census was a demonstration of Caesar's power: a single command issued in Rome had repercussions that reached around the known world. And it was a reminder that no one could ever hope to challenge imperial authority.

Yet it was in *those days* that hope entered the world. It was in *those days* that the definitive basis for all hope stepped in and began the revolution. And it was in *those days* that God assured his people that he wasn't finished, it wasn't over—in fact, it was only just beginning.

Many of us find ourselves living in *those days*. It may not be imperial oppression or the dismantling of the faith community—though, for many of our sisters and brothers in Christ around the world, it is exactly those things. For others of us, *those days* may be days of sickness, of marital trouble, of financial hardship, or so much more. It's essential that we not compare our suffering with that of others because, whatever *those days* look like, they can be painful, crippling, even devastating. *Those days* can take a thousand different forms, but what they all have in common is that they seem to exclude the possibility of hope. Yet we will find, as did the people of God more than two millennia ago, that God does some of his best work in the most hopeless of situations.

So we can have a sure and certain hope that it's not over for us. God is not finished in our situations or our circumstances. He's not through in his work in us and for us. However oppressive *those days* may seem, our God is greater. *Those days* do not eliminate our hope. Instead, they create the perfect conditions for us to lean into the hope of God's promise to one day heal, redeem, and restore all creation.

Questions for Reflection or Discussion

What hopeless days in your own life might be called "those days"?

_____

_____

_____

_____

_____

_____

When you've experienced despair and hardship in your life, what things—large or small—happened in the midst of that time to bring you hope?

_____

_____

_____

_____

_____

_____

What brings you hope today?

_____

_____

_____

_____

_____

_____

Prayer

Write a prayer of hope.

_____

_____

_____

_____

_____

_____

_____

_____

Whose Mother Was . . .

Scripture

MATTHEW 1:1, 3, 5–6

This is the genealogy of Jesus the Messiah the son of David, the son of Abraham: . . . Judah the father of Perez and Zerah, whose mother was Tamar, Perez the father of Hezron, Hezron the father of Ram . . . Salmon the father of Boaz, whose mother was Rahab, Boaz the father of Obed, whose mother was Ruth, Obed the father of Jesse, and Jesse the father of King David. David was the father of Solomon, whose mother had been Uriah's wife.

One of the many things that distinguishes the Bible from other ancient literature and mythology is that it never attempts to present its heroes without their flaws. The greatest champions of the faith so often made such a dreadful mess of it all. They doubted and denied, betrayed and abused, lied and cheated. The Hall of Faith in Hebrews 11 could just as accurately be called a Rogues Gallery. Yet the Bible makes no attempt to cover up the stains or sugarcoat reality. On the contrary, it shines a light on the parts we would tend to leave in shadows, bringing into sharp focus these fragile heroes with their feet of clay as a celebration of God's gracious ability to bring beauty out of dust and hope out of ashes.

The genealogy of Christ is the same. Surely, we would assume, if an exception could be made, it would be here! Surely this is where Matthew the evangelist could skip over some of the sordid details—not lie, just *omit* some of the more scandalous parts of Christ's lineage. Alexander the Great claimed the demigod Hercules as one of his ancestors; Julius Caesar insisted that his family was descended from the goddess Venus. Ancient heroes and rulers emphasised the greatness and grandeur of their family trees. They shone light on the glory of their bloodlines. Here, Matthew is introducing the King of all kings and Lord of all lords—it's the perfect place for him to do some pruning on the family tree! Instead, he puts special emphasis not on the heroes but on the scandals. He shines his spotlight on the parts of the tree we would seek to cover up.

Tamar—the victim of family politics and the predatory sexual instincts of her father-in-law— is included in the genealogy of Christ. This woman, who was abused and betrayed and left to fend for herself in an unfriendly world—something that culture in that time period would've considered a source of shame for her—is highlighted and elevated to a place of beauty and emphasis as one of the links in the chain that brought the Saviour into the world.

Rahab and Ruth are both recorded. Rahab was a prostitute—not acceptable in the eyes of the people of God, yet she was revered because she once helped the Israelites escape from a hostile military situation. Afterward, they took her in and allowed her to live among them as one of them. Ruth was a foreigner too—and not just any foreigner but one of the worst kinds: a Moabite. The Israelites had laws against comingling with foreigners, yet God also expected them to make exceptions from time to time, and Ruth was one such exception. She was an outsider brought into the community of God's people to become one of them.

Uriah's wife—better known to us today as Bathsheba—also makes the genealogy list. Bathsheba was another victim of a powerful man. King David's refusal to control his lust led to a series of events that eventually saw him betray one of his own subjects, having him killed. This culture in this time period would consider David's acts to be a source of shame for his victim. Yet here Bathsheba ascends to a place of honour in this genealogical record of how hope came to save the world.

There are seasons when we find ourselves in messes we have either inherited or made. It can be difficult to find hope, to believe that things will ever improve, that light could ever dawn in this place of darkness.

But the genealogy of Jesus is a clear message to the people of God about the way God brings hope out of ashes and light out of darkness. We can sometimes be tempted to think that redemption is just something that happens to some deep-down, hidden-away part of us that will one day fly away to glory. But our God is making all things new, and he's doing it right now. He's redeeming every inch and corner of creation. So, whether we have brought this disaster on ourselves, or it's been inflicted on us by others, he is more than willing and more than able to redeem it and bring hope out of even this. Just ask Tamar or Bathsheba or Rahab or Ruth.

Questions for Reflection or Discussion

What do you think about the claim that the Bible never attempts to present its heroes without their flaws?

_____

_____

_____

_____

_____

_____

_____

_____

_____

_____

How does the inclusion of "messy" in the genealogy of Jesus offer us hope today?

_____

_____

_____

_____

_____

_____

_____

_____

_____

Prayer

Write a prayer about the messy situation in your life that you need Jesus to redeem.

_____

_____

_____

_____

_____

_____

_____

_____

_____

_____

_____

How Will This Be?

Scripture

LUKE 1:34–38

"How will this be," Mary asked the angel, "since I am a virgin?"

The angel answered, "The Holy Spirit will come on you, and the power of the Most High will overshadow you. So the holy one to be born will be called the Son of God. Even Elizabeth your relative is going to have a child in her old age, and she who was said to be unable to conceive is in her sixth month. For no word from God will ever fail."

"I am the Lord's servant," Mary answered. "May your word to me be fulfilled." Then the angel left her.

I've always loved a happy ending. I know it's perhaps not the most artistic way for a story to end; I know it's not always the most insightful or profound, or even the most realistic—but I just can't help it. I'm a simple man. I want to see the couple living happily ever after; I want to see conquered villains and triumphant heroes. I want it all to end well. But the *best* stories don't make it easy. They make you work for it. They bring you through the darkest valleys before they let you see the brightest lights.

In the cinematic adaptation of J. R. R. Tolkien's *The Two Towers*, the two heroes Sam and Frodo have reached a crisis point in their quest. The odds seem insurmountably stacked against them. Their enemies are too many and too strong, and their mission is too vast for two simple hobbits from the Shire. Frodo tells his companion, "I can't do this, Sam."

And his loyal friend replies, "I know. It's all wrong. By rights we shouldn't even be here. But we are. It's like in the great stories, Mr. Frodo. The ones that really mattered. Full of darkness and danger, they were. And sometimes you didn't want to know the end because how could the end be happy? How could the world go back to the way it was when so much bad had happened? But in the end, it's only a passing thing, this shadow. Even darkness must pass. A new day will come. And when the sun shines, it'll shine out the clearer. Those are the stories that stayed with you. That meant something, even if you were too small to understand why. But I think, Mr. Frodo, I do understand. I know now! Folk in those stories had lots of chances of turning back—only they didn't. They kept going because they were holding onto something."

Frodo asks, "What are we holding onto, Sam?"

Sam says, "That there's some good in this world, Mr. Frodo. And it's worth fighting for."

Sam's right. In the end, it's all worth it because, even in the deepest darkness, there's incredible, impossible hope. God's people have built their lives upon the fact that no word from God will ever fail, even when it's impossible. Even when there's no way things could ever get better, there's hope. Even when we can never get past this, there's hope. Even when they will never come home, there's hope. Even when that relationship can never be mended, there's hope—because no word from God will ever fail.

Mary was a teenager, doubtless with her own dreams and plans for the future. Then Gabriel appeared to disrupt all that and tell her she had a part to play in God's plan. This simple peasant girl from the middle of nowhere suddenly had a role in the redemption and renewal of all creation. It would mean loss; it would mean shame; it would mean whispers and rumours about the girl who became pregnant outside of marriage. Yet, even from this darkness and trouble and pain, Mary clung to the impossible hope that God would use it for the ultimate and perfect good. God would use it to carry the good news of life and freedom to the very ends of the earth, ensuring that all could be part of the wonderful celebration God was preparing.

We may find ourselves in the sad part of the story, in the hard part of the story. We may find ourselves in the place where hope seems ridiculous or even impossible. Nevertheless, no word of God will ever fail, although we may have to wait a long time to see God's promises fulfilled. God has assured his people that he is always at work for our good, even when it seems there's no way. He has assured us that he specialises in bringing life out of death and light out of darkness.

We are never hopeless. Light will always dawn for the people of God eventually. It may not happen when we want or in the way we expect, but God is faithful and trustworthy. He's the One who goes before, behind, and beside his people. The One who assured Mary assures us today.

Questions for Reflection or Discussion

What do you think about the author's comparison of our hope in Christ to the scene from *Lord of the Rings*? Is the comparison a good one? Why or why not?

_____

_____

_____

_____

_____

_____

_____

_____

What does it mean that "no word from God will ever fail"?

_____

_____

_____

_____

_____

_____

_____

_____

_____

_____

Prayer

Write a prayer about the word from God you are waiting to be fulfilled in your life.

_____

_____

_____

_____

_____

_____

_____

_____

_____

_____

_____

_____

Light Shines in the Darkness

Scripture

JOHN 1:1–5

In the beginning was the Word, and the Word was with God, and the Word was God. He was with God in the beginning. Through him all things were made; without him nothing was made that has been made. In him was life, and that life was the light of all mankind. The light shines in the darkness, and the darkness has not overcome it.

In C. S. Lewis's story *The Lion, the Witch and the Wardrobe*, the enchanted realm of Narnia is ruled by the White Witch, a tyrant whose magic keeps the land trapped in a perpetual winter. When a young English girl named Lucy finds herself in a snow-covered Narnian forest, she meets a faun named Mr. Tumnus. As he shares the stories of his world with her, he speaks quietly of the White Witch: "It is she that has got all Narnia under her thumb. It's she that makes it always winter. Always winter and never Christmas; think of that!"

In the UK, Christmas falls at the coldest, darkest time of the year, within days of the winter solstice—the shortest day of the year. Many people leave for work in the dark and return home in the dark. We might see brief patches of light and life, but creation itself seems to be sleeping. The leaves have fallen, the grass won't grow, and so many animals have vanished. We can very easily feel like Mr. Tumnus—that it's always winter and never Christmas.

We are certainly not the first to feel this way. The history of ancient Israel often felt like relentless winter. They suffered as slaves in Egypt for four hundred years. They were exiled in Babylon for decades. By the time of Christ, they were yet again suffering under the oppression of foreign rule; they lived in their own home yet were still exiles. Through it all, they had been waiting for a Saviour, a Messiah, one who would set it all right again. It surely felt like it was always winter, always dark, without any hope of light.

But John assures us that, even in the midst of the long, cold darkness, the light shines and has not been overcome; it *will* not be overcome; it *cannot* be overcome. And that light is so bright and warm and strong that it's worth waiting for through the long, cold winters of our soul—whatever form those take and whatever disguises they wear. Our circumstances and situations cannot overcome the light of Christ.

However challenging and difficult they may be, however painful and unbearable they may feel, even however undeserving we may be, our Light shines in the darkness, and he cannot be overcome by loneliness or fear or anxiety, by loss or grief or unemployment. Christ's light shines in the deepest darkness. It may be winter, but Christmas is coming.

Questions for Reflection
or Discussion

What does it mean to believe that the light cannot be overcome by the darkness?

_____

_____

_____

_____

_____

_____

_____

_____

_____

What does the phrasing "always winter and never Christmas" signify?

_____

_____

_____

_____

_____

_____

_____

_____

_____

When have you seen light in a dark place? What were the circumstances? How did the light and the darkness interact with each other? How did seeing the light make you feel?

_____

_____

_____

_____

_____

_____

_____

_____

_____

_____

Prayer

Write a prayer about the ability of light not to be overcome by darkness.

_____

_____

_____

_____

_____

_____

_____

_____

_____

_____

_____

And They Were Terrified

Scripture

LUKE 2:8–9

And there were shepherds living out in the fields nearby, keeping watch over their flocks at night. An angel of the Lord appeared to them, and the glory of the Lord shone around them, and they were terrified.

We often have a tendency to romanticise certain things. Nature is peaceful and serene and beautiful—until we have to spend a night in a tent in the middle of nowhere. Then every noise becomes a monster and every pebble under the pillow becomes a razor-sharp boulder.

So it is with shepherds in the Bible. We can easily imagine these folks to be the salt of the earth—humble farmers looking after their flocks, at one with nature and one another and the world around them. Yet Scripture hints that this perspective is not always shared by characters in the salvation story.

Even the future king David was treated with nothing but scorn by his own family. His father seemed to forget he even existed because he was always off looking after what his brother later called "those few sheep" (see 1 Samuel 17:28). The truth is, Jewish shepherds commanded little respect from their community. Not good enough to follow a rabbi, their work with flocks and herds meant these high school dropouts were unable to maintain the strict ritual cleanliness laws demanded by the religious leaders. By every estimation, shepherds were amongst the last people God could be expected to visit with such incredible news. For God to entrust *those people* with a revelation like this would've been unimaginable. Shepherds had no position or power or status; no way of being good enough or doing well enough; they were quietly despised by their peers and openly rejected by the religious establishment. They had no qualifications, no spiritual status, no hope. They were perpetually left out and left behind.

Yet God chose to send a choir of angels to *these people* to bring a message of universe-shaking, life-transforming, shepherd-saving hope. They were the very first to learn that Messiah had been born, that light had dawned, that hope had come at last. And it was a hope that included even them. Today, too, it's a hope that doesn't exclude, doesn't set entry requirements, doesn't have a minimum standard for behaviour or education or finances or anything else we could imagine. Jesus Christ offers hope to every single person, regardless of who they are or what they've done or where they've been. And this hope transforms those who receive it.

The shepherds didn't simply return to their work with the flocks as if nothing had happened. Instead, they "spread the word concerning what had been told them about this child" (Luke 2:17), and they went around "glorifying and praising God for all the things they had heard and seen" (Luke 2:20). These shepherds became the very first gospel missionaries, telling anyone who would listen about the new hope that had been given to them and to the entire world.

The hope that Christ brings reaches even us. However unlikely it may seem, however undeserving we may be, it reaches us right where we are, even if we're sitting on a hill watching sheep. The hope of the gospel includes all of us, and it transforms all of us.

Questions for Reflection or Discussion

Who are the ancient shepherds of our world today—those who might be entrusted with the message of Jesus but whom the rest of society might view as outcasts or unimportant or nuisances?

_____

_____

_____

_____

_____

_____

_____

_____

What does God's choice of messenger tell us about what God expects of us?

_____

_____

_____

_____

_____

_____

_____

_____

_____

Prayer

Write a prayer of confession and repentance for the times when you ignored a message from God because of the "packaging" it came wrapped in.

_____

_____

_____

_____

_____

_____

_____

_____

_____

_____

_____

_____

_____

_____

_____

_____

_____

_____

_____

_____

_____

_____

Light Has Dawned

Scripture

ISAIAH 9:2

The people walking in darkness have seen a great light; on those living in the land of deep darkness a light has dawned.

Our family has a number of Christmas Eve traditions. One of the most important is taking a family walk through the village. We wrap up warm and take the dog for a stroll around the community, enjoying the decorations and trying to decide which house has our favourite display. There's something beautiful about how, on this dark, cold, wintry evening, we take time together to focus on the light and beauty that isn't snuffed out by the darkness but instead shines all the brighter.

In Isaiah 9, the prophet is preaching to people who will soon suffer defeat and be carried into exile, where they will languish for seventy years. When this prophecy finally comes to its fulfilment in Christ, Israel is in bondage in their own home, in their own land, suffering under Roman occupation. Yet in this very darkness, the light of God's promise shines with inextinguishable radiance. When there was no hope, when there was no help, when there was no way out and no way through, the Lord stepped in, as only he could—and he still does.

In our place of deepest darkness, when we're utterly at the end of ourselves, when all of our resources have run out and all of our hopes have run dry, the light of Christ still shines, and it can never and will never be overcome.

The exile in Babylon didn't extinguish his light; the disappointment of returning home to torn-down walls and a temple of rubble didn't extinguish his light; conquest by Rome didn't extinguish his light; not even all the power of sin and death could snuff out this divine light that shines all the brighter the darker things get.

In some way, we still await the final and ultimate fulfilment of this promise given through Isaiah because we still live in a world that can be deeply and painfully dark. But we wait in sure and certain hope that one day, the light of Christ will fill and flood and saturate every inch and corner of creation, and darkness will be driven out and driven away for the very last time, never to return again.

This season of Advent isn't just about waiting and preparing to celebrate the *first* coming of our Lord; it is also intended to turn our hearts and minds to the second and *final* coming, when all those walking in darkness will see a great light as the sun of righteousness rises with healing in its rays.

So take heart! This darkness will not endure. Our redemption draws near. As Paul tells us, "the night is nearly over; the day is almost here" (Romans 13:12).

Questions for Reflection or Discussion

When have you experienced light in the darkness (whether literally or metaphorically)?

_____

_____

_____

_____

_____

_____

_____

_____

_____

What does ragged hope look like? Hope that is found in the rubble, or in the midst of torn-down walls?

_____

_____

_____

_____

_____

_____

_____

_____

_____

Prayer

Write a prayer about ragged hope that persists in the darkness and the rubble.

Do Not Be Afraid

Scripture

MATTHEW 1:20

But after he had considered this, an angel of the Lord appeared to him in a dream and said, "Joseph son of David, do not be afraid to take Mary home as your wife, because what is conceived in her is from the Holy Spirit."

The Shawshank Redemption tells the story of a brutal New England prison, but it is ultimately a story about hope. An inmate named Red tells his friends that hope is a dangerous thing because it can drive you insane. Hope has no place in prison, he says, because you'll wait and wait for something better to arrive, and it never will.

Another prisoner, Andy, disagrees. "Hope is a good thing," he says. "Maybe the best of things."

Andy knows that when everything seems dark and we have every reason to despair, hope becomes most vital, most essential, most life-giving. There *will* be times when hope seems foolish, crazy, or even dangerous. Like Red, we can be tempted to bury our hope deep down because it seems to be setting us up for inevitable disappointment. But God often works in situations that seem the *most* hopeless, and we can be even more encouraged when God steps in and does the impossible.

God did it with Abraham. The New Testament tells us in two separate places that Abraham was "as good as dead" (Romans 4:19; Hebrews 11:12), yet God promised to make him a father of nations. To give birth to a family line that would bring hope to all creation, the Lord chose a couple who had been infertile for their entire marriage. There were numerous younger couples who were capable of bearing strong children and becoming nation builders, but God chose Abraham and Sarah, assuring them that this foolish hope would come to pass.

God did it with Moses. God used Moses to lead the people out of Egypt, out of the land of slavery, with incredible signs and wonders, then brought them right to the shore of the Red Sea. With water before them and Pharaoh's army behind, everything seemed lost. Surely God could have brought them by some other road? Yet he parted the sea and led the people through with a wall of water to their left and their right—the God of foolish hope.

God did it with David. He took a simple shepherd boy—forgotten by his father and despised by his brothers—and had him anointed king of Israel, assuring him he would lead his people to greatness.

And God did it with Joseph. The angel assured this simple carpenter that his young fiancée would conceive and give birth to the Son of God. God promised Joseph that the impossible would happen because God set his heart and mind upon it. As Paul would later say, "Let God be true, and every human being a liar" (Romans 3:4).

What was true for Abraham and Moses, what was true for David and Joseph, remains true for us today. He is still the God of foolish hope, the God who is able to do immeasurably more than all we ask or imagine, making none of the situations and circumstances of our lives hopeless or helpless.

The advertising for *The Shawshank Redemption* said, "Fear can hold you prisoner; hope can set you free."

However foolish it may seem.

Questions for Reflection or Discussion

What do you think about the author's claim that hope becomes the most essential at our darkest, most despairing moments? Why might you agree or disagree?

_____

_____

_____

_____

_____

_____

_____

_____

_____

How can fear become a method of imprisonment, and how would hope work against that?

_____

_____

_____

_____

_____

_____

_____

_____

_____

Prayer

Write a prayer of hope that entrusts your fears to God.

Second Sunday
of Advent

peace

DECEMBER 7, 2025

Scripture

So Joseph also went up from the town of Nazareth in Galilee to Judea, to Bethlehem the town of David, because he belonged to the house and line of David. He went there to register with Mary, who was pledged to be married to him and was expecting a child. While they were there, the time came for the baby to be born, and she gave birth to her firstborn, a son. She wrapped him in cloths and placed him in a manger, because there was no guest room available for them.

At times, Christmas can seem like the least peaceful time of year. Anyone who has ever left their Christmas shopping to the last moment can testify to that! Yet even when all the planning and preparations are complete, many of us still find very little peace. Between wrapping and cooking, family meals and family fights, and accommodating out-of-towners, peace seems to be a rare commodity.

We can, perhaps, find some comfort in the fact that a lack of peace is perfectly in keeping with the very first Christmas. Finding peace in the midst of chaos may well be the oldest Christmas tradition we have.

Joseph and Mary had already spent months facing the problems and struggles that come from a suspicious pregnancy in a small and rural community. Now they had to travel all the way to Bethlehem to register for the Roman census—around an eighty-mile journey, which would have taken at least four days. Then they arrive in Joseph's ancestral hometown only to discover that the crowd had beaten them. Bethlehem was full to bursting with travellers, and the only place they could find to deliver Mary's child was literally fit for animals. There seems to have been little room for peace in their Christmas, just as there often seems to be little room for it in ours—because soul-deep peace cannot be *found*; it has to be *accepted*.

Joseph and Mary undoubtedly experienced the peace they desperately needed when they held the newly born Son of God. Even amidst all the chaos of the pregnancy and the journey and the delivery, there can be no doubt that they felt the peace that can only come from God when they heard and saw and held their baby—their Saviour.

Peace cannot be bought at a store or ordered online. It cannot be gift-wrapped or served on a plate. However hard we strive, however much we do, the peace we most desperately and urgently need has its source in Jesus Christ. The peace of God is a gift of God's grace, freely given to all who do as Jesus's earthly parents did—simply be in his presence. The chaos may not cease. The holy family eventually had to flee Bethlehem because a tyrant plotted the murder of every male child in the area in a futile attempt to kill the Messiah.

Our chaos may continue, and it may even increase. After the miraculous and incarnational birth of the Christ, Mary, Joseph, and baby Jesus were refugees in another country for a time before they could safely return home. But the chaos of a broken world cannot diminish or spoil the peace that God gives. It cannot overcome or overwhelm the peace that comes from sitting at the feet of Jesus. Christ promised us unmatchable peace (see John 14:27). To paraphrase the old song, "We've got peace that the world can't give, and the world can't take it away."

Questions for Reflection or Discussion

Does it comfort you, as the author suggested, to realise that the first Christmas was probably not a very peaceful one? Why or why not?

_____

_____

_____

_____

_____

What does the author mean by the statement that "soul-deep peace cannot be found; it has to be accepted"?

_____

_____

_____

_____

_____

If Jesus is the source of our peace, and if we are Christians who follow Jesus but we don't feel at peace, what can we do to bring the peace of Jesus to ourselves? (Think about the difference between finding and accepting peace.)

_____

_____

_____

_____

_____

Prayer

Write a prayer asking God to grant you peace in a situation where you need it.

_____

_____

_____

_____

_____

Through the Holy Spirit

Scripture

MATTHEW 1:18

This is how the birth of Jesus the Messiah came about: His mother Mary was pledged to be married to Joseph, but before they came together, she was found to be pregnant through the Holy Spirit.

The Christian band Casting Crowns has a song named "Dream for You." The second verse imagines God speaking to Mary: "Hey Mary, I've heard you've been dreaming, making plans for your big wedding day, but I've been thinking . . ."

Before they were visited by their angelic messengers, it's hard to imagine that either Mary or Joseph could have expected what God had in store for them. How could they have dreamed of the part they would play in salvation history, the contribution they would make to God's redemption story? Up until this point, their dreams must have been very similar to those of their peers and neighbours—an honest living, a loving family, as long and peaceful a life as they could manage together.

Then they received this commission from God to be parents of Messiah, mother and father to the One who would change everything. In an instant, their hopes and dreams for the life ahead of them changed dramatically. Many of us would resist or resent a call that required us to make so many sacrifices, to implement such dramatic changes to our lives. Within the next few years, Mary and Joseph relocated to Bethlehem, then fled to a new country as refugees, only to finally return to Nazareth once it was safe again.

Their quiet, peaceful life was rudely and dramatically interrupted. Yet we're given no clue in Scripture as to any resentment or bitterness on either of their parts. In fact, almost every time Joseph is mentioned in the book of Matthew, it is in the context of swift obedience.

The interruption of their peace was a light and momentary thing when weighed against the privilege of being such a major part of God's story. Their part wasn't always easy. In fact, not long after the birth, Mary was promised, "A sword will pierce your own soul too" (Luke 2:35). Their role in salvation history brought challenges and trials, pain and tears. But there is no hint that they ever regretted their choice. In fact, Mary was such a part of the story that she even stood at the foot of the cross, watching her beloved son die.

Following Christ along the way will often mean allowing our version of peace to be interrupted. It will often mean our plans being disrupted, our agenda being rewritten, even overruled. But Mary and Joseph are part of that great cloud of witnesses assuring us that it's always, always worth it. They would promise us that any sacrifice on our part is far outweighed by the infinite richness of following Jesus. They would encourage us that any peace we allow to be interrupted will be repaid ten thousand times over, and more besides.

Don't resist God's interruptions. Welcome them, embrace them, and allow him to take you further than you've ever imagined possible.

Questions for Reflection or Discussion

What do interrupted/readjusted plans mean to you? Are they upsetting and stressful, or do they not bother you much?

_____

_____

_____

_____

_____

_____

_____

_____

If you are the type of person who finds interruptions and changes to plans to be deeply stress-inducing, how might you be able to invite peace into the process next time it happens?

_____

_____

_____

_____

_____

_____

_____

_____

_____

_____

Why do you think God interrupts our plans sometimes?

_____

_____

_____

_____

_____

_____

_____

_____

_____

_____

Prayer

Write a prayer committing yourself to lean into the next interruption God brings into your life. (Careful—God has a habit of answering these kinds of prayers very quickly!)

_____

_____

_____

_____

_____

_____

_____

_____

_____

_____

_____

The Lord's Servant

Scripture

LUKE 1:38

"I am the Lord's servant," Mary answered. "May your word to me be fulfilled." Then the angel left her.

How do you manage in a crisis? When the bottom seems to be falling out of your world, when you feel like your whole life has caught on fire, how do you handle it? Some of us may panic—it's all overwhelming and feels like far, far too much for us to cope. Others may go into business mode and lock out any and all feeling until the crisis has passed.

But some of us may have been blessed to encounter those saints of God who—in the midst of storms and troubles and trials, in the midst of disaster and disappointment, in the midst of crises and catastrophes—remain firmly embedded in a deep, deep peace. They don't ignore the issues; they don't plunge into the river of denial; they don't bury their heads in the sand and hope it all blows over. They face the crises of life in a badly broken world with an unshakeable, immovable peace because they know they can trust God with their cares.

Peace is not blind optimism that things will work out; it's not jamming our eyes shut to block out the messiness of the world. It's the certainty that even here and even now, even in all of this brokenness and all of this darkness, God is still present and still working.

We see it in today's scripture with Mary. This teenage girl, confronted suddenly and without warning by one of heaven's messengers—a being of such glory that time and again throughout Scripture, their first greeting had to be, "Do not be afraid!"

Gabriel then told the girl that she would play an important role in salvation history. She would face scandal and suspicion from her neighbours; she would face the uncertainty of a fiancé who may or may not accept her. He told her that the child she would carry was the One for whom her people had yearned for centuries, the Saviour they'd anticipated for longer than anyone could remember. Her child will be the fulfilment of hopes and dreams that had been nurtured for generations. More than that, he wouldn't just be her son, but he would be the Son of God himself.

This was staggering and incredible news. Yet Mary's response was unhesitating, full of the peace that can only come from fully trusting in God.

Are we prepared to trust that the God of peace knows what is best? Are we willing to rest in the promises of Scripture that our days were written in his book before any of them came to be; that he is always working things together for the good of those who love him?

Our heavenly Father can always be relied upon. Even when we face realities that stagger us, that confuse us, and that threaten to terrify us, we can trust in the peace of God that transcends our understanding (see Philippians 4:7).

Questions for Reflection or Discussion

What's your crisis MO? How do you respond to frightening/troubling/ unsettling situations? Do you panic and become useless, or do you turn off all emotion and do what needs to get done and only allow yourself to fall apart later, when the situation is resolved? Or something else?

_____

_____

_____

_____

_____

_____

_____

_____

_____

Why do you think Mary was able to respond to Gabriel's message with such calm obedience?

_____

_____

_____

_____

_____

_____

_____

_____

_____

_____

What does it mean for you to experience peace in the midst of chaos?

_____

_____

_____

_____

_____

_____

_____

_____

_____

_____

_____

Prayer

Write a prayer asking God to bathe you in peace.

_____

_____

_____

_____

_____

_____

_____

_____

_____

_____

_____

_____

The Time Came

Scripture

LUKE 2:6–7

While they were there, the time came for the baby to be born, and she gave birth to her firstborn, a son. She wrapped him in cloths and placed him in a manger, because there was no guest room available for them.

Perhaps my favourite image of the birth of our Lord is a painting by Gari Melchers named *The Nativity*. The reason I find it so beautiful is that it is profoundly, uncomfortably *real*. It couldn't be more different from our Christmas card nativity scenes with all of their warmth and comfort and cosiness.

In this painting, the holy family are depicted in what appears to be a cold and barren, cellar-like space, Mary lying propped up against some cart wheels as she rests, presumably in the attempt to keep the cold and damp from sinking into her bones. Joseph sits awake and hunched over—to my mind, looking utterly terrified. Here is a man very aware of just how out of his depth he finds himself. Any new father may feel that way, but Joseph seems painfully aware that this helpless newborn is the Son of the living God, made flesh in a way that no one could ever have imagined. A water bowl and jar lie beside Mary, draped with a few rags. The delivery clearly happened right on the floor, in the most inauspicious way a king could possibly arrive.

It seems an utterly hopeless scene—except for one thing. In all of their exhaustion and concern, in all their wonderings about what the future holds for their young family, in all the chaos they've just faced and may well face in the future, both Joseph's and Mary's eyes are resolutely fixed on the single source of light in the entire painting—the manger holding the newborn Saviour. A terrified stepfather sitting beside a drained mother can find peace in, draw strength from, and have hope renewed by the One who lies wrapped in cloths, sleeping in a manger.

Jesus is literally the only bright spot in the scene.

Many of us can so easily feel like Joseph—out of our depth, barely keeping our heads above water, living in what an old Chinese proverb calls "interesting times," facing chaos today and uncertainty tomorrow. Peace seems elusive, even impossible.

Yet, for the people of God, Christ is present. He is always intimately, sufficiently present. And, like Joseph in the Melchers painting, we will find that Christ's light is enough to bring encouragement; his light is enough to strengthen and sustain; his light is enough to grant us peace.

So we can launch out again into a disordered world, into a restless world, into a world that seems designed and built to keep us in perpetual chaos. And in the midst of it all, we can be assured that we will make it. Like the disciples had to learn for themselves, Christ will never sink, however rough the storm, and if we are in his boat, we will not sink either. We may not be able to laugh at the storm—the disciples weren't laughing, and they literally had Jesus in the boat. But we can have an ironclad certainty that the storm will pass and that Jesus will be present with us in the midst of it.

When we are most in need of peace, our best course of action is to follow the example of Joseph in the Melchers painting: fix our eyes on Jesus, the pioneer and perfecter of faith, the One who gives peace when we need it most, right in the heart of the storm.

Questions for Reflection or Discussion

Google the Melchers painting referenced by the author in this devotional reflection, if you haven't already. Look at it. What do you see in the scene that is different from or similar to the things the author described?

_____

_____

_____

_____

_____

_____

_____

_____

It can be simple to say something like "fix our eyes on Jesus" as a metaphor. But what does that mean in a practical, literal sense? How can it bring us peace?

_____

_____

_____

_____

_____

_____

_____

_____

_____

Prayer

Write a prayer expressing your appreciation for God's incomprehensible peace.

_____

_____

_____

_____

_____

_____

_____

_____

_____

_____

_____

_____

_____

_____

_____

_____

_____

_____

_____

_____

_____

_____

_____

_____

_____

On Earth Peace

Scripture

LUKE 2:13-14

Suddenly a great company of the heavenly host appeared with the angel, praising God and saying, "Glory to God in the highest heaven, and on earth peace to those on whom his favor rests."

December 25, 1914, is perhaps one of the most famous Christmas Days in history. Known as the "Christmas truce," soldiers all along the Western Front of World War I climbed out of their trenches and crossed over No Man's Land to exchange prisoners, food, and even small gifts. They also sang carols, had joint burial services, and even played a famous football match.

One German officer recorded, "So after all, the Christmas festival—the festival of love—caused the hated enemies to be friends for a short time." Unfortunately, it truly was only for a short time. Within days the truce was a mere memory, and the increasingly bitter conflict had begun again. Indeed, the following year, as the war went on, such truces were fewer and rarer, and by 1916, they were all but nonexistent.

It has been estimated that, since 1939, there have been only twenty-six days of continuous, unbroken peace across this planet—and some scholars believe that figure to be optimistic.

Up until the twentieth century, there was a widespread belief that humankind was morally evolving and that, very soon, war would be obsolete and we would truly know peace on earth. In a horrifying refutation of that belief, the twentieth century was undoubtedly the bloodiest in human history, with two global wars and innumerable localised conflicts. Even at the time of this writing, conflict rages in Ukraine and the Gaza Strip, and various other places besides—perhaps even frighteningly close to the homes of those reading these words.

In light of all this human-generated violence, the angelic promise of peace seems laughable, insane, impossible; in fact, it may even seem offensive—until we realise that the peace of which the angels assure us is something far deeper and far higher than simply an absence of conflict between nations. This peace is even greater and more significant than good relations with those around us on a personal level.

The peace the angels promised with the birth of Christ is peace between God and the people God loves. It is the re-creation, the remaking, the re-forging of a relationship that was broken by the fall of humanity. It is the enabling, by grace, to live in union with God, no longer alienated from him, no longer running and hiding from him like Adam and Eve did. It is the knowledge that there is now no condemnation for those who are in Christ Jesus; the certainty that in his amazing love, lavished upon us, we should be called children of God; the absolute assurance that nothing we could ever face, nothing we could ever do, nowhere we could ever go will be able to separate us from the love of God that is in Christ Jesus our Lord.

This peace is not merely the absence of conflict. It's not a tenuous treaty signed between nations or a football match played between warring trenches. It is peace with God—the healing of a wound that stretches back to Eden, the restoration of that which was once so terribly broken. This peace is available in whatever circumstances we find ourselves, even if we are in the middle of a warzone. It can't be stolen from us, and we can't be excluded from it because it has been perfectly won for us by Christ.

Questions for Reflection or Discussion

Have you heard before about the Christmas truce during WWI? What are your thoughts on it?

_____

_____

_____

_____

_____

_____

_____

_____

_____

If peace is not simply an absence of conflict, then what is it?

_____

_____

_____

_____

_____

_____

_____

_____

_____

Sometimes those who work for peace are called "divisive." Is it divisive to work actively for peace? Why or why not?

_____

_____

_____

_____

_____

_____

_____

_____

_____

_____

Prayer

Write a prayer about the kind of peacemaker you would like to be.

_____

_____

_____

_____

_____

_____

_____

_____

_____

_____

My Eyes Have Seen

Scripture

LUKE 2:28–32

Simeon took [the child Jesus] in his arms and praised God, saying: "Sovereign Lord, as you have promised, you may now dismiss your servant in peace. For my eyes have seen your salvation, which you have prepared in the sight of all nations: a light for revelation to the Gentiles, and the glory of your people Israel."

People of a certain generation reading this devotional may be unable to remember the Stone Age—when computer games came on something called a "cassette tape." If you wanted to play a game, you had to be prepared for the long haul because loading could take as long as fifteen minutes! Today, we're used to instant gratification. Our food, our entertainment, even our commutes—we expect everything to happen *right now*. I can't be the only one who marks the point in a neighbouring queue where I would have been if I had only joined it, instead of the one I chose.

But Scripture encourages God's people to take the long view, reminding us that what we see and experience, what we suffer and endure, will not always be this way. Simeon had been waiting a long time. He saw the fulfilment of his hopes and his waiting in the Christ child, and he also knew there was more yet to come.

Things will not always be broken. They will not always be spoiled. We will not always have to live in a place of broken pieces and sharp edges. And we will not always live in a world where peace is rare, brief, and hard-won. There is coming a day when God's peace will flood all creation, when all that is will be saturated with perfect, cosmic peace. It will be peace with ourselves, peace with one another, peace with the created order, and—most wonderful of all—peace with God.

The Saviour who is the Prince of Peace has come into this world. Simeon recognized him in the temple. And there is also coming a day when the peace that Christ achieved through his victory on the cross will drive out and drive away everything that would diminish and destroy. So it's worth holding on. It's worth running our race with perseverance because the peace that Christ will one day usher in is worth it all.

The peace that God's people enjoy now, like Simeon—the peace that is available to all people, everywhere and everywhen—is only a deposit and foretaste of what is to come. Greater, deeper, eternal peace is on its way.

Questions for Reflection or Discussion

Have you ever gotten something you waited a long time for? How did it feel once you got it?

What does it mean to "take the long view" and accept that the world as it is now is not how things will always be?

_____

_____

_____

_____

_____

_____

_____

_____

_____

_____

Does the idea of taking the long view bring you hope or despair? Does it foster peace within you, or does it bring anxiety?

_____

_____

_____

_____

_____

_____

_____

_____

_____

_____

_____

Prayer

Write a prayer explaining to God how you feel about waiting.

_____

_____

_____

_____

_____

_____

_____

_____

_____

_____

_____

_____

_____

_____

_____

_____

_____

_____

_____

_____

_____

_____

_____

They Spread the Word

Scripture

LUKE 2:15–20

When the angels had left them and gone into heaven, the shepherds said to one another, "Let's go to Bethlehem and see this thing that has happened, which the Lord has told us about."

So they hurried off and found Mary and Joseph, and the baby, who was lying in the manger. When they had seen him, they spread the word concerning what had been told them about this child, and all who heard it were amazed at what the shepherds said to them. But Mary treasured up all these things and pondered them in her heart. The shepherds returned, glorifying and praising God for all the things they had heard and seen, which were just as they had been told.

We live in an age of spoilers. In case you're not familiar with the term, it's when someone reveals a major plot point of a movie, book, or TV show, ruining the experience for others. Some years ago, following the release of a highly anticipated novel, a number of individuals read its six hundred pages overnight simply so they could drape a huge banner from a bridge overlooking a busy motorway in the attempt to spoil the ending for unsuspecting motorists. Theologically speaking, people who do this are *the worst*. We don't rank sins by their level of heinousness, but if we did!

Even so, not all spoilers are wrong or evil. In fact, some spoilers are to be embraced and encouraged because some truths are so powerful, so wonderful, so revolutionary and world-changing and life-saving that they simply *must* be shared; they have to be spread as widely and quickly as possible. These are truths far more powerful and wonderful than how a movie or a novel ends. These are truths so eternally significant that the entire world needs to see and hear and experience them.

So it was with the message of peace that the shepherds carried. When they met the Christ child, Luke the evangelist tells us that "they spread the word concerning what had been told them about this child." And, as they left, they did so "glorifying and praising God for all the things they had heard and seen."

Spoiler alert: everything has changed! A new day has dawned, a new hope has arisen, a new peace is now possible!

Spoiler alert: the revolution has begun in a manger in Bethlehem! The entire world has changed overnight, and nothing will ever be the same again!

This was a message far too important for the shepherds to keep to themselves. They felt compelled to share it with any who would listen and with all whom they encountered. These simple herdsmen were the first ambassadors of the gospel: Messiah has come, the kingdom of God has drawn near, heaven has stepped down and touched earth and has brought peace!

We are inheritors of that message and that mission. Our world is desperate for peace. Kings and emperors, generals and premiers have all promised some variation of peace in our time, and this broken world has made liars of them all. But God's people are ambassadors of a peace that transcends understanding; a peace that transcends borders and boundaries; a peace that isn't won at the barrel of a rifle or the tip of a bayonet but is achieved through who Christ is and what he has done.

This is a message we cannot afford to keep to ourselves. So, by God's grace and with God's help, may each of us and all of us follow in the footsteps of the shepherd missionaries and spread the word concerning what we have seen and heard and experienced for ourselves.

Questions for Reflection or Discussion

What does it look like to spread the word of Christ's gospel today, in a world where everyone knows what Christianity is and everyone already has their own opinions about it?

_____

_____

_____

_____

_____

_____

_____

_____

_____

The author says, "Our world is desperate for peace." What does that mean? If the world really is desperate for peace, why don't we have it?

_____

_____

_____

_____

_____

_____

_____

_____

_____

Prayer

Write a prayer asking God to help you understand how to share the peace of Christ in a way that will be meaningful and useful to those around you.

_____

_____

_____

_____

_____

_____

_____

_____

_____

_____

_____

_____

_____

_____

_____

_____

_____

_____

_____

_____

_____

_____

_____

Third Sunday of Advent

joy

DECEMBER 14, 2025

Scripture

This is how the birth of Jesus the Messiah cam about: His mother Mary was pledged to be married to Joseph, but before they came together, she was found to be pregnant through the Holy Spirit. Because Joseph her husband was faithful to the law, and yet did not want to expose her to public disgrace, he had in mind to divorce her quietly.

———————

Children are often wonderful teachers, especially when they're receiving gifts. Most adults have learned how to express thanks and appreciation for even the most mundane and disappointing of presents:

"Socks! How did you know?"

"What an unusual jumper, thanks so much!"

"My goodness, what an interesting flavour this cake has; thank you for baking it yourself!"

Children, on the other hand, have often not learned this etiquette and are sometimes brutally frank in their assessment of such presents. If they are unhappy or uninterested, they often show little hesitation in expressing their true feelings.

Yet how often do the most unexpected things lead to the most joy? How often do the most unusual, seemingly uninteresting things bring the most pure and unbridled joy to our hearts? There's a reason clichés become clichés—because, more often than not, they're accurate. We've all seen (or been!) the child playing with the box more than with the toys it contained.

Joseph could not have been expecting much joy. Matthew presents this earth-shattering, reality-changing news in stark terms: "Before they came together, [Mary] was found to be pregnant." There's no sense of drama; no hint of the heartache, the disappointment, the anger Joseph must have felt at the news of this seeming betrayal. Joy must have been far from his mind and far from his heart.

The fact of the matter is, when we look at the first Christmas without the veneer of greeting cards and nativity scenes, it's a mess. Yet God redeemed it! From that mess he brought life, light, hope—he brought what many of us will remember singing once upon a time: "joy unspeakable and full of glory."

Many of us have messy lives. Many of us will even have a messy Christmas. But we know, as Joseph surely discovered, that God can weave that mess into a tapestry of surpassing beauty. He can redeem that mess and use it to bring inexpressible joy.

Our mess is not the end. God can take it and use it to bring us to a place that seems impossible and unreachable—a place of genuine, soul-deep joy.

———

Questions for Reflection or Discussion

What is something unexpected in your life that has led to deep joy?

_____

_____

_____

_____

_____

_____

_____

_____

_____

_____

Acknowledging, naming, and *feeling* our raw emotions is an important part of healthy and mature emotional intelligence in the life of an adult. When bad things happen to us, especially when they are surprises, *after* we have allowed ourselves to feel negative emotions about the situation, how can we then turn around and consider what joy might come without denying or dismissing or ignoring our valid negative emotions?

_____

_____

_____

_____

_____

_____

_____

_____

_____

Prayer

Write a prayer asking God to help you learn how to better hold joy in tension with your own negative emotions.

_____

_____

_____

_____

_____

_____

_____

_____

_____

_____

God with Us

Scripture

MATTHEW 1:22–23

All this took place to fulfill what the Lord had said through the prophet: "The virgin will conceive and give birth to a son, and they will call him Immanuel" (which means "God with us").

When our family moved house, we had to repeat the single most challenging building project of my entire life—our son's bed. This monstrosity had left me exhausted, sore, and frustrated when we first built it, and now we had to do it all over again. In spite of offers of help from our new church family, I was adamant we could do it ourselves. I was painfully, dangerously, embarrassingly *wrong*.

Human beings are built for community; we are built to be together. In fact, the very first thing the Bible ever declares to be "not good" is being alone—trying to get through life by ourselves. We are built for relationship—both with other humans and with God. Yet, when the fall of humanity occurred in the garden of Eden, that perfect relationship with God was broken, almost irrevocably. *Almost.*

Jesus Christ is *Immanuel*—"God with us." He is God living in our flesh and walking in our shoes; he is God facing a badly broken world; He is God moving into our neighbourhood and making his dwelling amongst us. God in Christ is literally moving heaven and earth to restore that perfect, intimate relationship. His heart has never been distance but always intimacy; it has never been separation but always union.

We can see this purpose reaching its perfect fulfilment and completion in Revelation 21:3: "And I heard a loud voice from the throne saying, 'Look! God's dwelling place is now among the people, and he will dwell with them. They will be his people, and God himself will be with them and be their God." And it's all the result of what we call the incarnation: God becoming flesh at Bethlehem; God becoming *Immanuel*.

Through this miracle of grace, the human family can once again know the joy of being in relationship with God; the joy of being his and knowing he is ours; the joy of having God with us, wherever we are and whatever we face. This is something prophets and priests and kings dreamed of and prophesied about for millennia. It's something our spiritual ancestors in the Old Testament longed for and pointed toward, and it's something that is perfectly fulfilled in Christ.

When we face the troubles and storms of life—and we will—we can know that Christ is *Immanuel*; he is with us. When we face difficult decisions and difficult people, he is with us. Joys are all the sweeter because he is *Immanuel*; sorrow can be endured because he is *Immanuel*. Loneliness is eased because he is with us; burdens can be borne because he is with us.

It's not about our good behaviour or our most strenuous efforts; it is simply because of who he is. God became *Immanuel* in his amazing grace and extravagant love; he remains with his people and for his people for exactly the same reason. It's not about how lovable *we* are; it's about the fact that *he* is love. Even when we don't deserve it and even when we haven't earned it, he remains *Immanuel*; he remains with us. He remains the most basic and foundational reality of life for the people of God.

And that is reason for joy.

Questions for Reflection or Discussion

What does it mean to you that God became human for our sake?

_____

_____

_____

_____

_____

_____

_____

_____

_____

Why do you think God allows the world to go on the way it is? Why not just fix everything now?

_____

_____

_____

_____

_____

_____

_____

_____

_____

_____

_____

Prayer

Write a prayer asking for the assurance of God's nearness when your ability to experience joy feels threatened.

_____

_____

_____

_____

_____

_____

_____

_____

_____

_____

_____

_____

_____

_____

_____

_____

_____

_____

_____

_____

_____

_____

_____

He Will Save His People

Scripture

MATTHEW 1:21

She will give birth to a son, and you are to give him the name Jesus, because he will save his people from their sins.

By this point in Advent, expectations are reaching an explosive point in many homes. Excitement is building as certain family members watch the calendar with feverish intensity. We just can't wait for Christmas to finally arrive! The waiting seems to have gone on for an eternity—we've had to exert superhuman patience as one day crawls into another.

The people of God in Scripture could relate. As year merged into decade merged into century, Messiah *still* hadn't arrived. This hero who would change everything, who would set everything straight and make everything right, this figure prophesied and expected literally from moments after the fall in Eden, still hadn't arrived.

Expectations were varied. Some expected a warlord in the mould of David—a conqueror who would drive out the Romans and restore Israel to its place of glory. Others imagined a priest-king or a custodian of the Mosaic law—someone who would perfectly fulfil all the legal requirements of righteousness. Still others envisaged some mysterious figure emerging out of nowhere, or a herald of the end of all things.

In truth, when Messiah came, he was unlike anything most people expected, but he was everything that everyone needed. He didn't come to do anything as trivial as secure a military conquest; he didn't come with fire and brimstone; he didn't take the throne in Jerusalem and usher in religious reform—a truth worth remembering in an age when Christians are tempted to rely on legislation and legislators to usher in the kingdom.

No, when Messiah finally came, he came to accomplish that which was most desperately and urgently needed. He came to do the work that no one else could do but that everyone, everywhere, painfully needed. He came to win the only victory that mattered and to defeat the only Enemy that counts.

Jesus came to save his people from their sins.

Note, he didn't just come to save us *in* our sins; he didn't save us to go *back* to our sins or to go *on* in our sins. No, he came to do a work so complete, so perfect, so once-and-for-all that those who trust in him and walk with him along the way can be saved, utterly and completely, *from* their sins. So that we can be saved from the power and dominion of sin right here and right now, no longer living as enslaved, as Christ warns in John 8:34, but can instead be truly, fully *free*.

The name "Jesus" is from the same Hebrew root as "Joshua," which can help us understand just how complete is the victory he has won for us. Like Joshua, Christ came to lead his people into the inheritance promised to us so long ago. He came to triumph fully over enemies far too big and far too strong for us to handle. He came to tear down walls and drive out that which would destroy us, and he asks us to choose for ourselves, even this very day, whom we will serve.

Christ brings us the joy of a victory we could never achieve for ourselves; the joy of a freedom we could never win for ourselves; the joy of being once and for all saved from our sins.

Questions for Reflection or Discussion

How has Jesus acted in opposition to your expectations of him in your life?

_____

_____

_____

_____

_____

_____

_____

_____

_____

What should be our response when Jesus acts in ways we don't expect?

_____

_____

_____

_____

_____

_____

_____

_____

_____

Prayer

Write a prayer expressing your trust in Jesus to confound expectations for the sake of the gospel.

_____

_____

_____

_____

_____

_____

_____

_____

_____

_____

_____

_____

_____

_____

_____

_____

_____

_____

_____

_____

_____

_____

My Spirit Rejoices

Scripture

LUKE 1:46-49

And Mary said: "My soul glorifies the Lord and my spirit rejoices in God my Savior, for he has been mindful of the humble state of his servant. From now on all generations will call me blessed, for the Mighty One has done great things for me—holy is his name."

One of my favourite TV shows is *The West Wing*. In one episode, a character named Leo tells the story of a man who fell in a hole. A doctor walked by, and when the man cried for help, the doctor wrote out a prescription and dropped it into the hole. The man's priest walked by, and when the victim again cried for rescue, the priest wrote out a prayer and dropped it into the hole. But when a friend of the man walked by, he leapt into the hole!

The first man said, "What are you doing?! Now we're both stuck in this hole!"

And his friend replied, "Ah, but I've been here before, and I know the way out."

Sometimes the best thing we can do for our loved ones is to be mindful of them in their suffering—to jump into the hole with them. Knowing that someone is with us, someone is for us, someone *sees* us, can make all the difference in the world. For a few verses in the book of Job, the prophet had the best friends in the world because they simply sat with him in the ruins of his life without saying a word. Things only went wrong once they began to speak.

Mary's song, known as the *Magnificat*, is an acknowledgement that things in the world are not right. The rich get richer, and the poor get poorer; corruption is rife, and abuse is rampant. Things have been broken, things have been twisted, things have not been the way they ought to be. We're in a hole, and we seem to be utterly trapped. But the *Magnificat* is nevertheless an expression of praise and a song of worship because God has been *mindful*. God is deeply aware and intimately involved. God is present in the pain of his people; he is active in their suffering. And his mindfulness—his seeing us—means that when he does act, he always does so perfectly.

God in Christ leapt down into the hole beside us. We can hear echoes of Exodus 3:7–8: "The Lord said, 'I have indeed seen the misery of my people in Egypt. I have heard them crying out because of their slave drivers, and I am concerned about their suffering. So I have come down to rescue them . . .'"

In Mary's time, God was mindful of the Roman occupation. God was mindful of the contempt in which his people were held. God was mindful of the fact that his temple had been despoiled and his law mocked. God was mindful that things were broken. But more than this, God was mindful that the Romans were the least of the problems facing creation. God's universe itself was twisted and spoiled, damaged and off course. Sin and death—never a part of his design—were a cancer that poisoned everything. But God was *mindful*. And in his mindfulness, God acted. In his mindfulness, God moved. In his mindfulness, God stepped in to bring life, freedom, joy.

J. R. R. Tolkien described Christianity as the ultimate fairy tale, partly because it has the ultimate happy ending. In Christ, the divine playwright wrote himself into his play to change the story, to bring about a happier ending than anything we could ever have imagined or brought about on our own. As God was mindful of the suffering of his people in Egypt, he was mindful of their suffering under Rome. As God was mindful of the suffering of all creation under the poison of sin, so he is mindful of our suffering; God is mindful of *your* suffering.

And in his mindfulness, God has acted and will act and is acting right now. And he will bring joy.

Questions for Reflection or Discussion

What do you think about the story of the two friends in the hole? Is it helpful or not helpful for them both to be stuck in the hole? Why or why not?

_____

_____

_____

_____

_____

_____

_____

_____

_____

_____

_____

_____

_____

_____

What does it mean to you to think of God as "mindful" of you and of your circumstances and, more broadly, of the world's circumstances?

_____

_____

_____

_____

_____

_____

_____

_____

_____

_____

Prayer

Write a prayer thanking God for God's mindfulness of you and asking God to help you be mindful of others in the same way.

_____

_____

_____

_____

_____

_____

_____

_____

_____

_____

_____

Great Joy for All the People

Scripture

LUKE 2:10–12

But the angel said to them, "Do not be afraid. I bring you good news that will cause great joy for all the people. Today in the town of David a Savior has been born to you; he is the Messiah, the Lord. This will be a sign to you: You will find a baby wrapped in cloths and lying in a manger."

For so many of us, Christmas is a time of incredible happiness. It's a time for family, for gifts, for food; it's a season of light in the midst of darkness, a time of celebration in the midst of the cold. Many of us, perhaps even most of us, have innumerable reasons for happiness in the Christmas season.

But this happiness is not universal. There are many others whose thoughts will be dominated this Christmas not by those seated around the table but by the chairs that are empty chairs—those to whom we've had to say goodbye and those we never got to meet. There will be those whose trees are not surrounded by gifts; those who struggle to keep the house warm through the long, dark nights. Some will struggle with their mental health around this special season or with the mental health of those they love. There are many, many reasons why people may not know the happiness that is expected around Christmas. That's why it is so important for us to realise that happiness and joy are not the same thing.

Happiness depends upon *happenings*. When life is good, when our circumstances are favourable, when our situations are positive, we know happiness. We're happy because we're not facing struggles or trials; we're happy because the road is smooth and the seas calm. But when storms come, when the path is hard, when we're facing the giants of life, it is only natural for us to lose that sense of happiness.

If we're lonely this Christmas, we don't need to feel strange that we're not euphoric with happiness. If we're grieving the loss of a loved one; if we're facing challenges in our finances or our health; if we're not sure what the new year will bring, or if we're regretting the decisions we've made throughout the past year, then it's only natural that this happiness is absent. And that's okay—because joy is far richer than simple happiness.

Joy comes from a spring far deeper than situations and circumstances. True joy is rooted in something outside ourselves and beyond the challenges and trials of life. The joy that can only come through our life in God and his life in us—the joy that is freely offered because of all that Christ has done and given—is available to us all.

The angel didn't proclaim a message of happiness or promise an easier life. He didn't assure the shepherds of an end to Roman oppression or a newfound respect from their neighbours. The angel didn't promise that they'd be *happy*. The angel promised *joy*, and he assured them that it was for *all* people, everywhere and everywhen. He assured them that this deeply rooted and foundational joy was being poured out lavishly from the heart of God and that it was all because of the baby being born in Bethlehem. It had nothing to do with happiness or happenings. It wasn't because things were getting easier or because the shepherds had developed a more positive outlook on life. It was because of who God is and what God had done.

Our joy can be solid as a rock this Christmas, regardless of where we find ourselves and what we're facing—not because of situations or circumstances but because Christ is born in Bethlehem, and he brings his people joy.

Questions for Reflection
or Discussion

What is the difference between happiness and joy as you understand it?

_____

_____

_____

_____

_____

_____

_____

_____

_____

_____

When or how have you found joy in situations that are, by all accounts, unhappy situations?

_____

_____

_____

_____

_____

_____

_____

_____

_____

Prayer

Write a prayer asking God to help you understand joy in a deeper way, and perhaps even to be a bringer of joy to others during unhappy circumstances.

You Who Are Highly Favored

Scripture

LUKE 1:28

The angel went to her and said, "Greetings, you who are highly favored! The Lord is with you."

There has never been anyone in all of salvation history, even in their lowest and vilest moments, who has been unloved by God. God's relentless, incessant, ironclad love reaches queens and paupers, tyrants and monsters. God's love fills and floods and saturates every inch of his creation. In short, there is nothing *special* about being loved by God. In one sense, it is the most ordinary and commonplace thing imaginable—we are one tree in an immeasurably vast forest that is *adored* by God.

Yet, as I grow older, I begin to wonder if, perhaps, God is able to love us *as if* we were special. Perhaps his love is so perfect; perhaps his grace is so amazing; perhaps his kindness is so awesome that he is able to look upon each and every one of us and call us his special friend. My first pastor used to say, "I don't know if God has favourites, but he seems especially fond of me." God is such a perfect Father that he doesn't pick and choose whom he loves, nor to whom he shows his love.

In Matthew 5:45 Jesus assures us that God's goodness to us does not depend on our righteousness: "He causes his sun to rise on the evil and the good, and sends rain on the righteous and the unrighteous." God is good to all! So good, in fact, that every single one of us should feel like we are God's favourite; so good that all of us should feel like Gabriel's greeting to Mary is addressed to us—we are highly favoured!

God may not play favourites, but in his wisdom and kindness, he is able to treat every one of us as though we were his special friend. And this is surely cause for constant and indescribable joy. Surely we are highly favoured.

Questions for Reflection or Discussion

If God doesn't play favourites, then what does it mean for us to be highly favoured?

_____

_____

_____

_____

_____

_____

_____

_____

_____

If God doesn't play favourites, then why was Mary told that she was highly favoured?

_____

_____

_____

_____

_____

_____

_____

_____

_____

Prayer

Write a prayer expressing your gratitude for God's fondness of you.

Just As He Promised

Scripture

LUKE 1:51–55

He has performed mighty deeds with his arm; he has scattered those who are proud in their inmost thoughts. He has brought down rulers from their thrones but has lifted up the humble. He has filled the hungry with good things but has sent the rich away empty. He has helped his servant Israel, remembering to be merciful to Abraham and his descendants forever, just as he promised our ancestors.

Confession time. There is a petty streak in me, of which I am not proud. When I notice a particularly aggressive driver on the road, weaving in and out of lanes, driving so close to the car in front that it seems as if they want to climb into the backseat, I keep an eye out for them at the next traffic jam we encounter. And my heart leaps with joy when I notice that all of their aggression, all of their dangerous driving, all of their selfishness has earned them precisely *nothing*. It's petty, I know. But it's also immensely satisfying.

Lord Jesus Christ, have mercy on me, a sinner.

But I believe this tendency in myself testifies to something deep within us all that rails against injustice. There is something embedded in the human heart that resents unfairness, cries out against it, resists it, and seeks to rectify it—whether it's as petty as aggressive driving or something much deeper, much more serious, much more real.

We know in our bones that injustice is unnatural. It's not the way the world is meant to be. We instinctively know that it goes against the grain of the universe; it's out of step with the way creation is intended to function. All over the world, people of all faiths and none mobilise to combat injustice in all of its shapes and forms. Whether it's poverty or illiteracy, human trafficking or addiction, physical or substance abuse, people all over the world organise to end it, prevent it, make it right. In the UK alone, there are more than 168,000 registered charities—because, whether we know God or not, whether we're part of his church or not, his grace is already at work in us, teaching us the simple fact that injustice is unnatural and has to be opposed.

Mary's *Magnificat* reminds us that God's coming kingdom is one of perfect, universal justice. Those who set themselves up above and beyond others will be brought low, and those who have been oppressed and trampled will be lifted high. Those who have filled their lives with riches at the expense of others will find their storehouses empty, whilst those who have been scraping by will find their cups overflowing. The wounded will be healed, the lonely will be set in families, the hungry will be fed, and perfect, cosmic, eternal justice will finally be done.

That day is coming, and the incarnation means that the first rays of dawn can already be seen. The kingdom will come in all of its brilliance at the end of the age, and its seeds are already bearing fruit in the world today. They can be seen anywhere God's people follow the command of the Lord through the prophet Micah to "act justly and to love mercy and to walk humbly with your God" (Micah 6:8). These seeds can be seen when we put into practice the words of the martyred German pastor Dietrich Bonhoeffer and "drive a spoke into the wheel [of injustice] itself."

Whether it's issues of race, education, inequality, sexuality, or any of the innumerable ways injustice rears its vile head, God's people are called and commanded to be on the cutting edge of opposing it.

And we can know a soul-deep joy at the fact that there is coming a day of perfect, universal justice for all. As Dr. Martin Luther King Jr. said, the arc of the moral universe is long, but it bends toward justice.

Questions for Reflection or Discussion

Are you familiar with the Dr. King quote about justice? What are your thoughts on it?

_____

_____

_____

_____

_____

_____

_____

_____

What should be the response of Christians to vast injustice in the world?

_____

_____

_____

_____

_____

_____

_____

_____

_____

_____

Sometimes Christians like to tell one another to keep their politics out of their faith. Yet Mary's *Magnificat* is quite political. What should be the role of politics in one's faith?

_____

_____

_____

_____

_____

_____

_____

_____

Prayer

Write a prayer about injustice.

_____

_____

_____

_____

_____

_____

_____

_____

_____

_____

**Fourth Sunday
of Advent**

love

DECEMBER 21, 2025

Scripture

JOHN 1:14

The Word became flesh and made his dwelling among us. We have seen his glory, the glory of the one and only Son, who came from the Father, full of grace and truth.

The Bible is many things. It's the story of a couple who became a family that became a nation that gave birth to a movement that would transform the world. It's a book about flawed and fragile people who fail and fall, who stumble so completely that it seems there's no way out and no way back yet who are nevertheless used by a God who is always greater than our greatest failures. It's a book that teaches us who God is and what God is like—and therefore who we are and what our lives are to be like. It's a book that shows us the way of light and life and teaches us to reject and renounce the way of darkness and death.

The Bible is so much, but at its heart, above and beyond anything else, before and after everything else, it's a book about relationship. It's the story of a King who desperately loves his people; a Father who longs for intimacy with his children, and who acts conclusively and decisively, at immeasurable cost to himself, to restore that intimacy and renew that relationship.

The staggering truth at the heart of holy Scripture is that God *wants* us. He is willing to move heaven and earth to be near us. He is willing to leave the throne of heaven, gladly laying aside the robes of majesty and honour and glory, all so he could become *Immanuel*—God with us.

God doesn't need us to complete him. He is perfectly fulfilled without us. From before time began, God existed in the loving community of the holy Trinity. He doesn't need us to satisfy him. But he loves us so much that he invites us into his already perfect fellowship. He draws us into that Trinitarian dance of Father, Son, and Holy Spirit. He pulls out a seat at the table and invites us to sit down and feast.

It's an incredible thought that God *wants* to be with us. When we were yet unlovely, unloving, and unlovable, nevertheless he set his heart and mind upon us. He drew near to us so we could draw near to him.

I once asked a member of our church, "Have you ever considered the simple truth that God enjoys your company? That he wants to spend quality time with you? That it's not a chore or a burden or an obligation—but that he delights in it?"

That's the way it was always intended to be. Before the fall of humanity, the Lord God would come down and walk with Adam and Eve and talk with them. He would share himself with them and allow them to share themselves with him. Even though his knowledge was perfect and his power complete, he still allowed these oh-so-limited beings to enjoy relationship with him.

And the entirety of salvation history has been about restoring that damaged relationship, recreating that lost intimacy, renewing that broken fellowship.

God doesn't need us, but he wants us so desperately that he always takes the initiative, always makes the first move, always speaks the first word. He loves us in a way that is so great, so staggering, so impossible, that he became human and *made his dwelling among us*. Or, as Eugene Peterson puts it in his translation of John 1:14, God moved into the neighbourhood—all for love of us.

Questions for Reflection or Discussion

Do you agree or disagree with the idea that the Bible is ultimately a story about relationship? Why or why not?

_____

_____

_____

If God doesn't need us, and if we tend to mess up God's plans just by being ourselves, why do you think God chooses to be in relationship with us?

_____

_____

_____

_____

_____

_____

_____

_____

Prayer

Write a prayer about the relational aspect of God's character.

_____

_____

_____

_____

_____

_____

_____

_____

_____

_____

_____

_____

_____

_____

What the Lord Commanded

Scripture

MATTHEW 1:24

When Joseph woke up, he did what the angel of the Lord had commanded him and took Mary home as his wife.

Some of us may remember the '90s hit "Teardrop" by the musical group Massive Attack. The opening lines went, "Love, love is a verb, love is a doing word."

Massive Attack would, perhaps, have been surprised to discover what gifted theologians they were because, on one level, this is a perfect way to describe biblical love. It's not an abstract concept; it's not a feeling; it's not something that comes and goes with our mood. No, scriptural love is as sure and strong as gravity. In the Bible, love is the first and last word in every conversation between God and his created world. Love is the driving force in salvation history, and it is always active, always moving, always doing.

Every time Joseph appears in the Gospel of Matthew, he perfectly demonstrates this truth. He makes three major decisions in the opening chapters. The first is here in chapter 1, where he obeys the command of God and takes Mary as his wife. The next two are in the following chapter: he takes his young family to Egypt to escape Herod's massacre and later he returns to Israel and settles in Nazareth. Both of these decisions follow the same pattern as chapter 1—the Lord spoke to Joseph in a dream, and Joseph got up and obeyed.

Joseph's love for God wasn't something vague or abstract. It wasn't a concept or an idea. It was rock solid, and it was active. The truth is, it can never be anything else—for him, or for us. Genuine love will always result in action. Like Joseph, our love for God and for neighbour will always compel us to get up and act, to get up and work, to get up and move.

The action doesn't save us; our obedience doesn't earn us more of God's favour, more of his blessing. Our loving service is always a *response* to what God has already done and what he has already given.

What action is love inspiring us to take in our own lives? How is our love for God and for neighbour compelling us to work, to move, to give? If our love doesn't express itself in action, if it doesn't inspire our words and our deeds, we have to ask ourselves: how genuine is it?

God's people are called and commanded to love him with our whole heart, soul, mind, and strength, and to love our neighbour as ourselves. This love will never be contained in a Valentine's card. It will always be expressed through our hands and feet, our time and money, in our work and our family life. It will always express itself in who we are and what we do. It will flow from us into the world around us as we follow Joseph's example and get up and put our love into action.

This action may be costly. *Doing* love is always harder than *feeling* love. But it's always worth it.

Joseph's love led to his being a link in the chain of salvation history. May we, like him, get up and allow our love to express itself in those countless little ways that together will change the world.

With apologies to Massive Attack, love isn't *only* a verb; it's also, in grammatical terms, a proper noun because the most perfect way we can understand love is that it is a Person. His name is Jesus.

Questions for Reflection or Discussion

What does it mean for love to be a verb rather than an emotion that we feel?

_____

_____

_____

_____

_____

_____

_____

_____

What action is love inspiring you to take in your life?

_____

_____

_____

_____

_____

_____

_____

_____

_____

Prayer

Write a prayer asking God to help you understand more deeply the character of love as *action*.

_____

_____

_____

_____

_____

_____

_____

_____

_____

_____

_____

_____

_____

_____

_____

_____

_____

_____

_____

_____

_____

_____

_____

_____

Outwitted

Scripture

MATTHEW 2:1–2, 7, 12, 16

After Jesus was born in Bethelehem in Judea, during the time of King Herod, Magi from the east came to Jerusalem and asked, "Where is the one who has been born king of the Jews? We saw his star when it rose and have come to worship him." . . . Then Herod called the Magi secretly and found out from them the exact time the star had appeared. . . . And having been warned in a dream not to go back to Herod, they returned to their country by another route. . . . When Herod realized that he had been outwitted by the Magi, he was furious, and he gave orders to kill all the boys in Bethlehem and its vicinity who were two years old and under, in accordance with the time he had learned from the Magi.

Part of the purpose of including the Magi in the incarnation story is to show that the gospel is never, ever exclusive. Prevailing thought said that when Messiah came, he would come as the saviour of the *Jewish* people, and they would finally be elevated to their rightful place above all others. The Magi show us that from the very beginning of the life of Christ on earth, his message was for *all* people. His love is so extravagant that it cannot be limited or contained.

The love of God always draws, always invites, always embraces. It makes room at the table for us—whoever we've been, whatever we've done, however we've failed or fallen. And if that love welcomes *us*, if it embraces *us*—how could we think to exclude anyone else? How could we think to deny anyone else the same welcome we've received? How could we think we have the right to shut the door in someone's face when that same door has been flung wide open to draw us in?

We all know people who are not easy to love. Herod was not easy to love. Considered a brutal tyrant by his peers, his slaughter of the boys in Bethlehem was very much in character. He murdered members of his own family, including his wife, in order to secure his reign, so killing peasant children he had never met would not have bothered him in the least.

Herod was unlovely; by any reasonable measurement, he was *unlovable*. Yet Christ came for Herod's sake too. Christ lived, died, rose again, ascended into heaven, and will one day return to make all things right *for Herod*—and for all the Herods of the world.

God loves the unlovely and the unlovable. He loves those who seem to go out of their way to escape his love, to render themselves outside his love, to make themselves immune to his love.

That means there's hope for all the Herods in our lives—even if it turns out those Herods might be ourselves. There's hope for all of us! We have all been guilty of unloveliness. Through word or thought, feeling or deed, we have all proven our inadequate, misdirected, disordered love. We have lived what Martin Luther would call lives curved in on ourselves. Yet we remain utterly, desperately loved by God.

No one is beyond the reach of God's love. No one has done too much or gone too far or fallen too low. There is always room in the story of salvation—because there is always room in the heart of God—for people like me, and you, and Herod. God's love is for all of us, and it is for all of them—even our enemies and opposites and irritants.

Questions for Reflection or Discussion

Think about the adage that those who need love the most often ask for it in the most unloving ways. What makes us capable of loving unlovable people? Why try at all?

_____

_____

_____

_____

_____

_____

_____

_____

_____

When have you been the unlovable person (perhaps even the Herod) in someone else's life?

_____

_____

_____

_____

_____

_____

_____

_____

_____

Prayer

Write a prayer asking God to help you learn how to recognize and offer love to those deemed unlovable.

_____

_____

_____

_____

_____

_____

_____

_____

_____

_____

_____

_____

_____

_____

_____

_____

_____

_____

_____

_____

_____

_____

_____

_____

_____

Between Your Offspring

Scripture

GENESIS 3:14–15

So the L ORD God said to the serpent, "Because you have done this, cursed are you above all livestock and all wild animals! You will crawl on your belly and you will eat dust all the days of your life. And I will put enmity between you and the woman, and between your offspring and hers; he will crush your head, and you will strike his heel."

It seems utterly, painfully dark. Everything seems completely, hopelessly broken. Adam and Eve fell for the lie that every human after them has also believed—that we can be the centre of our own universe, the captain of our own fate, the master of our own soul; that we can be full and complete and satisfied on our own and by ourselves; that we can be big enough and strong enough to sit upon the throne of our own lives. And, as it always has and only ever can, it ended in disaster for them.

Sin entered the world and, through sin, death. Everything was broken. Like drowning people, Adam and Eve thrashed about, desperate to grab anything that might save them, but instead they dragged all of creation down with them.

In this moment of utter despair, we are given the very first promise in Scripture that a Saviour is coming. Things will not always be broken; sin will not have the last word; death will not have the final say. This is the very first assurance that God has not given up, has not walked away, has not turned his back on us and, in fact, never will. God will pursue his wayward children relentlessly.

This promise, given moments after creation broke, assures us that the brokenness is temporary. Sin is a foreign intrusion into God's world. It's been rightly observed that beauty is more original than sin. It *has not* always been this way, and it *will not* always be this way.

The long night of weeping, of pain, of loss, of separation from God and from one another, is not a forever thing. There is coming a day when the one who has helped break everything will himself be broken. The enemy of our soul will receive a crushing blow from which there will be no recovery.

And the waiting is *hard*. That's partly what this season of Advent is about—learning to wait well and to anticipate with eagerness the dawning of that day, when the kingdom of God comes in all its fullness and everything that has been so dark will be illuminated with a light of unimaginable brilliance.

All of God's people find themselves in what Dr. Seuss called "the waiting place," and for some of us it's harder than others. For some of us, the broken edges of a fallen world seem sharper than usual, and they can cut deep.

But it will not always be this way. Someday, the sun will set for the last time, and we will shed our last tear. Someday, death will claim its last victim, and everything that is crooked will be set straight, and everything that is broken will be mended.

The wait may be long, but it is worth it. As any child on Christmas Eve can tell us—the joy of the morning makes the long wait worthwhile.

Questions for Reflection or Discussion

Today's scripture sounds quite depressing and even has the word "curse" in it, but the author says it contains a promise. What is the promise held in Genesis 3:14–15?

_____

_____

_____

_____

_____

_____

_____

_____

_____

What is the hardest thing for you about waiting?

_____

_____

_____

_____

_____

_____

_____

_____

_____

Prayer

Write a prayer about waiting.

_____

_____

_____

_____

_____

_____

_____

_____

_____

_____

_____

_____

_____

_____

_____

_____

_____

_____

_____

_____

_____

_____

Scripture

REVELATION 22:20–21

*He who testifies to these things says, "Yes, I am coming soon."
Amen. Come, Lord Jesus. The grace of the Lord Jesus be with
God's people. Amen.*

———

It's often been observed that Christians live in the tension of the now and the not yet.

Death has been swallowed up in victory—but for now we still live in a broken world.

God has won, is winning, and will win—but for now we still endure the sharp edges and broken pieces of a world that just doesn't work right.

Today, we celebrate the fact that Christ has come! As our Eastern friends remind each other when they celebrate Christmas Day, Christ is born; glorify him!

Yet we still live in anticipation of that day when he will return in absolute, undeniable triumph.

Christmas Day is a wonderful day of celebration, of joy, of love, and of life. But we can live in sure and certain confidence that it is only the foretaste of what lies ahead for God's people.

As C. S. Lewis put it, when we compare Christmas Day to that day, it is only "the scent of a flower we have not found, the echo of a tune we have not heard, news from a country we have never yet visited."

That reality also brings incomparable hope to those for whom Christmas Day may be tinged with sorrow, with pain, with grief—because we are pressing on to a day when every tear will be wiped away by the hands of God himself; when every wound will be utterly and perfectly healed; when everything sad and broken and spoiled is finally restored and redeemed, once and for all.

Wherever this day finds us, may we remember that it is only the first-fruits of what lies ahead.

Christ is born; glorify him!

Amen. Come, Lord Jesus.

Notes